D1286672

SPECTACLED BEARS

by Tammy Gagne

AMICUS HIGH INTEREST AMICUS INK

Amicus High Interest and Amicus Ink
are imprints of Amicus
P.O. Box 1329, Mankato, MN 56002
www.amicuspublishing.us

Library of Congress Cataloging-in-Publication Data

Gagne, Tammy, author.
  Spectacled bears / by Tammy Gagne.
      pages cm. -- (Wild bears)
  "Amicus High Interest is published by Amicus."
  Summary: "Presents information about South America's spectacled
bears, their forest habitats, and their distinctive fur patterns."-- Provided
by publisher.
  Audience: K to grade 3.
  Includes bibliographical references and index.
  ISBN 978-1-60753-778-6 (library binding)
  ISBN 978-1-60753-877-6 (ebook)
  ISBN 978-1-68152-029-2 (paperback)
  1. Spectacled bear--Juvenile literature. [1. Bears.] I. Title.
  QL737.C27G326 2015
  599.78--dc23
                         2014043618

Photo Credits: Bildagentur Zoonar GmbH/Shutterstock Images, cover;
NaturePL/SuperStock, 2, 18; Ammit Jack/Shutterstock Images, 5, 23; C.
Huetter/Corbis, 6; Tui De Roy/Minden Pictures/Corbis, 9; Pete Oxford/
Minden Pictures/Corbis, 10, 22; Roland Seitre/Minden Pictures/Corbis,
13; SuperStock/Glow Images, 14; Christian Hütter/ImageBroker RM/Glow
Images, 17; Paul S. Wolf/Shutterstock Images, 21

Produced for Amicus by The Peterson Publishing Company
and Red Line Editorial.

Designer Becky Daum
Printed in Malaysia

HC 10 9 8 7 6 5 4 3 2 1
PB 10 9 8 7 6 5 4 3 2 1

TABLE OF CONTENTS

WHERE IN THE WORLD?

Spectacled bears live in South America. They live in the forests of the Andes Mountains. Some people call them Andean bears.

Fun Fact

The spectacled bear is the only bear that lives in South America.

6

WEARING GLASSES

The bears' fur is mostly dark. Many bears also have light fur on their faces. This is where their name comes from. They look like they wear **spectacles**.

SHY BEARS

Spectacled bears stay far from people. They live high in mountain forests. They sometimes climb down to find food. The bears are **nocturnal**.

EASY TO PLEASE

Spectacled bears eat many things. They mostly eat fruits and plants. The bears also eat bugs and birds. They even eat cactuses!

MAKING NOISE

Spectacled bears are noisier than most bears. They make sounds to each other. Sometimes they screech loudly. Other times they purr softly.

MARKING TERRITORY

Male bears rub against trees. This leaves their **scent** behind. Then other males know the **territory** is taken.

SMART CLIMBERS

Spectacled bears are great climbers. They are also smart. The bears use sticks to build platforms. This lets them reach food high off the ground.

Fun Fact
Spectacled bears sleep in trees.

BEAR FAMILIES

Cubs stay with their mother for a year. They ride on her back. She sometimes carries them instead. She uses one paw to hold them. The mother can run on her other three legs.

Fun Fact

Spectacled bears can live up to 25 years.

AT RISK

Not many spectacled bears remain. Farmers have taken over much of their **habitat**. Hunters have killed many bears. It is now against the law to hunt spectacled bears.

21

SPECTACLED BEAR FACTS

Size: 132–441 pounds (60–200 kg), 51–79 inches (130–200 cm)

Range: South America

Habitat: mountains

Number of babies: 2

Food: fruits, plants, insects, birds

WORDS TO KNOW

habitat – a place where a plant or animal naturally lives

nocturnal – active at night

scent – smell

spectacles – a pair of eyeglasses

territory – an area where an animal lives and eats

LEARN MORE

Books

Dolson, Sylvia. *Bear-ology: Fascinating Bear Facts, Tales & Trivia.* Masonville, Colo.: Pixy Jack Press, 2009.

Swanson, Diane. *Bears.* Vancouver, British Columbia: Whitecap Books, 2010.

Websites

Wildlife Conservation Society—Andean Bear
http://www.wcs.org/saving-wildlife/bears/andean-bear.aspx
Learn more about the dangers faced by spectacled bears in the wild.

World Wildlife Fund—Spectacled Bear
http://wwf.panda.org/about_our_earth/species/profiles/mammals/spectacled_bear
Read about what people are doing to help spectacled bears.

INDEX